All you need to create a world is some crayons. Hare and Bear have a whole box of colored crayons and lots of ideas. In this book they show you how to draw a tree. If you watch how Hare and Bear do it, you can draw one too. Just copy the shapes from the colored box at the top of each page onto your own drawing. And soon you'll be swinging in the branches.

Hare and Bear Draw A Tree

Diann Timms

Reader's Digest Kids
Pleasantville, N.Y.–Montreal

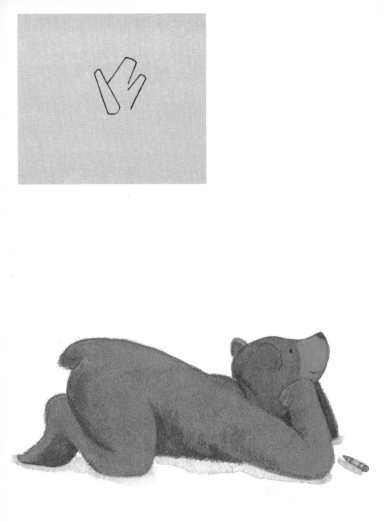

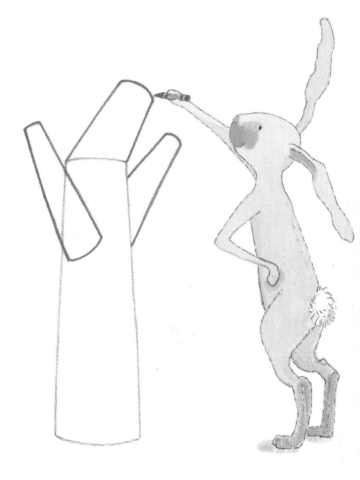

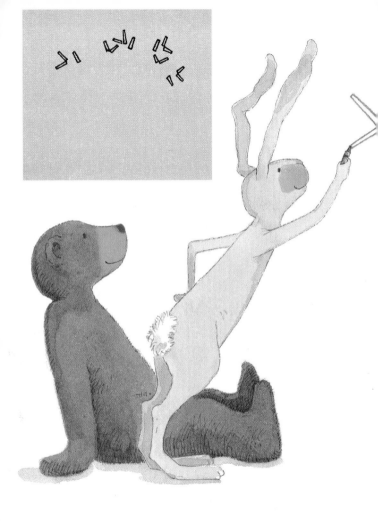

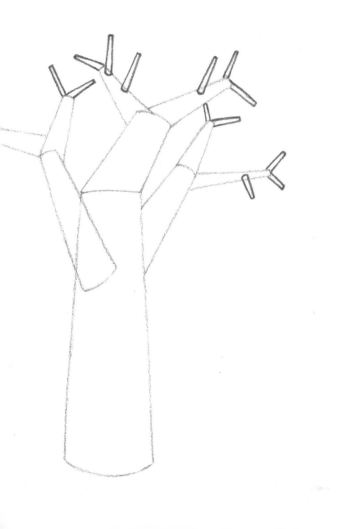

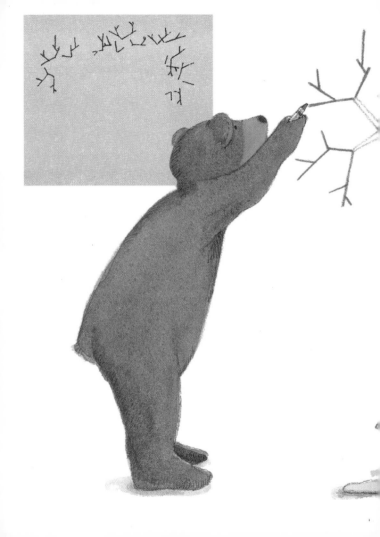

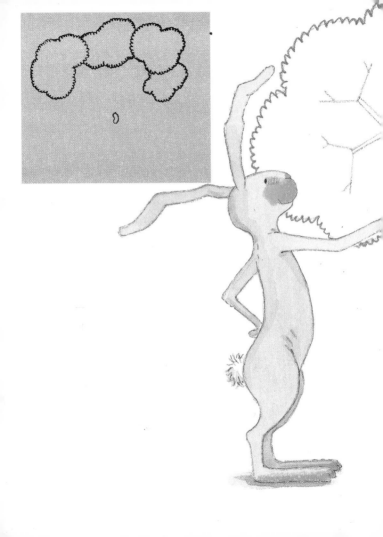

What shall we draw next?

A Reader's Digest Kids Book

Conceived by Diann Timms and Delian Bower Publishing

Copyright © 1993 Diann Timms

rights reserved. Unauthorized reproduction, in any manner, is prohibited.

Library of Congress Cataloging in Publication data applied for.

ISBN 0–89577–530–1 (v. 4)

ISBN 0–89577–548–4 (set)

Printed in the United States of America

99 98 97 96 95 94   10 9 8 7 6 5 4 3 2 1